Pineapple Pleasures: 60 #Delish Pineapple Recipes

RHONDA BELLE

Copyright © 2016 Rhonda Belle

All rights reserved.

ISBN-13: 978-1540494894

ISBN-10: 1540494896

DEDICATION

To Foodies Everywhere...Enjoy & Be Well!

Table of Contents

Palate-Pleasing Pineapple 8
    Abigail's Pineapple Pound Cake 8
    African Pineapple & Peanut Kale Stew 9
    African Spinach & Zucchini Sauté with Pumpkin Seeds & Dried Pineapple 9
    Agave Teriyaki 10
    Asian Island Sausage & Meatball Bites 10
    Avocado & Pineapple Salad 10
    Boned Pork Loin with Pineapple Cream Sauce 11
    Caramelized Pineapple 11
    Coconut Chicken with Pineapple Mango Salsa 12
    Coconut Tofu with Spicy Pineapple Chutney over Rice 12
    Cuban Caramel Pineapple Flan 13
    Easy Island Salsa 13
    Exotic Pineapple Beachside Martini 14
    Fresh Pineapple Slaw 14
    Granny's Pineapple Cake 15
    Grilled Pineapple and Onion Salsa 15
    Happy Hummingbird Cake 15
    Hawaiian Baked Beans 16
    Hawaiian Chicken Salad 16
    Hawaiian Sweet & Sour Vegetables over Rice 17
    Hibachi Pineapple Spears 17
    High Five Freeze 18
    Homemade Ginger Pineapple Sherbet 18
    Island Style Couscous Salad (Vegan) 18
    Jerk Sausage & Meatball Bites 19
    Luau Salad 19
    Orange Pineapple Honey-Glazed Roast Pork 20
    Papaya Pineapple Strudel (Vegan) 20
    Pepper-Papaya-Pineapple Chutney 21
    Perfect Piña Colada 21
    Perfect Pineapple Fried Rice 21
    Perfectly Pineapple Vinaigrette 22
    Pickled Pineapple 22

Pineapple and Cantaloupe Melon Drink 22
Pineapple and Coconut Shake 22
Pineapple Chess Pie...23
Pineapple Chili Juice 24
Pineapple Citrus Chutney 24
Pineapple Coconut Yum Yum...24
Pineapple Cooler 25
Pineapple Cucumber Mint Smoothie 25
Pineapple Key Lime Spritzers 25
Pineapple Li Hing Mui...25
Pineapple Marmalade 26
Pineapple Mimosa..26
Pineapple Mint Cooler...27
Pineapple Sherbet..27
Pineapple Truffles 27
Pineapple Upside-Down Cake 28
Pineapple-Brown Sugar Glazed Chicken Breasts...28
Pineapple-Coconut Milk Drink 29
Polynesian Paralysis 29
Pressed Cuban Ham and Pineapple Sandwiches 29
Rosy Fruit Cocktail..30
Rum, Mango, and Pineapple Relish...30
Slow-Cooker Sweet and Sour Sticky Ribs 30
Spiced Pork Tenderloin with Pineapple Salsa 31
Taiwan-Style Vegetable Wraps with Spicy Pineapple Sauce 32
Tropical Spice Pork Tacos 32
White Crème Pineapple Rum..33

To the love of my life, Johnny.
You are Mommy's greatest inspiration.

To my Mom & Dad (Sunset February 2016)
Love you both...always!

Palate-Pleasing Pineapple

Nothing puts you in a tropical or summery mood faster than the sweet taste of fresh pineapple! Not only is it naturally sugary and delicious, pineapple can benefit personal health. High in vitamins and minerals, one healthy ripe pineapple fruit can supply about 16% of daily requirement for vitamin C – a potent antioxidant. Pineapples are also high in malic acids that help boost immunity, promote smooth and glowing skin and healthy bones. Perfect for refreshing fruit snacks, entrees, sauces, smoothies, desserts, salsas, and mixed drinks, pineapples offer good taste that's good for you! Try these 60 great recipes for palate-pleasing pineapple experiences every time. Enjoy!

Abigail's Pineapple Pound Cake
½ teaspoon baking powder
½ teaspoon vanilla
1 ½ cups all-purpose flour
1 ½ cups granulated sugar
1 cup diced pineapple
1 cup pineapple juice
1 teaspoon salt
5 eggs
8 ounces butter, plus more for greasing tin
confectioners' sugar for dusting
Rum glaze (optional, recipe below)

Put butter in a large, deep bowl, and beat with an electric mixer at medium until the texture is soft and pliable. Add sugar, and continue mixing at medium-high until mixture turns pale and fluffy and sugar is completely incorporated, about 4 to 5 minutes. To this mixture, add eggs one at a time beating well for about 45 seconds after each egg is added. Scrape the bowl once in a while. Preheat the oven to 350 degrees. Next, sift flour with salt and baking powder. Beat flour into the egg mixture at low, a little at a time. Alternate adding pineapple juice and diced pineapple with the flour. Add the vanilla extract toward the end, and continue to beat tat low speed until ingredients are combined. The resulting batter should have a smooth texture. Pour mixture into a greased loaf tin, and bake in oven for about 1 hour, or until toothpick inserted into center comes out clean. Remove from oven, let cool sprinkle with confectioners' sugar or rum glaze. *To make the rum glaze*: Melt ½ cup butter in a small pan over medium heat. Stir in ½ cup brown sugar and ½ cup white sugar. Bring to a gentle simmer for about 5 minutes, and stir in 1 cup of rum. Cook for another 5 minutes, until all sugar has dissolved. Gently poke holes in the cake with a fork and pour glaze evenly over entire cake. #Delish!

African Pineapple & Peanut Kale Stew

½ cup chopped fresh cilantro
½ cup chunky peanut butter
½ cup vegetable broth or water, plus additional as necessary
½ teaspoon crushed red pepper flakes
½ teaspoon salt
1 medium red onion, chopped
2 large garlic cloves, finely chopped
2 tablespoons peanut oil
4 cups chopped fresh kale
freshly ground pepper
Hot cooked rice
Hot red pepper sauce to taste
Two 8-ounce cans crushed pineapple in juice (undrained)

In a large deep-sided skilled with a lid heat oil over medium heat. Add onion and cook until lightly browned, 7 to 10 minutes, adding the garlic the last few minutes. Add pineapple and its juice, red pepper flakes, salt and black pepper; bring to a simmer over medium-high heat. Stir in kale, cover, and simmer over medium-low heat stirring occasionally, until kale is just tender, about 5 minutes. Stir in peanut butter, broth, and cilantro; simmer, uncovered, stirring occasionally, until the kale is tender, about 5 minutes. If thinner consistency is desired, add additional broth or water, as necessary. Serve warm, over rice, with hot pepper sauce passed separately. #Delish!

African Spinach & Zucchini Sauté with Pumpkin Seeds & Dried Pineapple

¼ cup chopped dried unsweetened pineapple
¼ cup unsalted raw pumpkin seeds, coarsely chopped
¼ cup vegetable broth
½ medium red onion, coarsely chopped
2 medium zucchinis, coarsely chopped
2 tablespoons canola oil or peanut oil
4 scallions, white and green parts, thinly sliced
One 6-ounce bag baby spinach
Salt and pepper to taste

In large nonstick skillet with a lid, heat oil over medium heat. Add onion and cook, until softened and fragrant, about 5 minutes. Add zucchini, scallions, pumpkin seeds, salt, and pepper; cook, stirring for 3 minutes. Add broth and pineapple, stirring to combine. Add spinach, tossing well to combine. Cover, reduce the heat to low, and cook, stirring a few times, until the spinach is just wilted and the zucchini is tender, about 5 minutes. Serve warm. #Delish!

Agave Teriyaki

¾ cup agave
1 can pineapple chunk
1 clove garlic minced
1 cup soy sauce
1 tablespoon grated ginger
2 pounds beef sirloin steaks cubed
green bell pepper cut into chunks
Whole water chestnut

Combine soy sauce, agave, ginger and garlic. Mix well. Pour over meat and marinate 4 to 8 hours, turning occasionally. Alternate meat on bamboo or metal skewers with water chestnuts, green pepper and pineapple chunks. Broil or grill to desired doneness. #Delish1

Asian Island Sausage & Meatball Bites

¼ cup honey
1 tablespoon ground ginger
2 tablespoons lemon juice
2/3 cup pineapple preserves
One 16-ounce package frozen cooked meatballs
One 16-ounce package small cooked smoked sausage links

In a 4-quart slow cooker combine pineapple preserves, honey, and lemon juice, and ginger. Stir in meatballs and sausage. Cover and cook on low for 4 to 5 hours or on high for 2 to 2 ½ hours. Serve immediately. Keep warm on low setting for up to 1 hour. Serve with toothpicks. #Delish!

Avocado & Pineapple Salad

½ cup dressing of your choice
1 medium pineapple
2 large, ripe avocados (soft to the touch)
Salt to taste

Peel and cut the avocados in half lengthwise, remove the pits, and cut flesh into ½ inch pieces. Peel the pineapple and cut fruit into ½ inch cubes. Mix both fruits in a salad bowl, and add the salt and dressing to taste. Garnish as you like, cover, refrigerate, and serve very cold. #Delish!

<u>Guava-Mint Vinaigrette (optional):</u>
¼ cup finely chopped fresh mint leaves
½ cup diced guava
¾ cup olive oil
1 teaspoon Dijon or yellow mustard
1 teaspoon onion powder
1 teaspoon parsley flakes
4 tablespoons white vinegar
Salt and pepper to taste
Sugar to taste

In a large bowl, combine vinegar, mustard, salt, pepper, sugar, onion powder, and parsley flakes. Whisk mixture for 1 to 2 minutes and continue to whisk while slowly dribbling in the olive oil or until the mixture thickens. Whisk in diced guava and mint. Then process in food processor or blender for about 1 minute. Refrigerate covered for about 30 minutes. #Delish!

Boned Pork Loin with Pineapple Cream Sauce
½ cup heavy whipping cream
1 onion, peeled and chopped
1 pork loin (about 3 pounds), boned, rolled, and tied
1 teaspoon Dijon mustard
1 teaspoon dried thyme
2 cups cubed fresh pineapple
4 tablespoons butter
Salt and pepper to taste

Preheat oven to 375 degrees. Untie the pork loin and trim off the skin and fat. Lay it flat, skin side down, and sprinkle and rub thyme, salt, and pepper all over the loin. Roll up the loin again, and retie it up with string. Place on a rack in a baking pan. Place the pan in the oven and bake for about 2 hours, or until well cooked. While loin is roasting, melt butter in a saucepan and add the onion and pineapple. Cook over very low heat for about 25 minutes, until very soft. Remove from the heat, and allow the mixture to cool slightly. Transfer to a food processor or blender, and add the cream and mustard. Process or blend until smooth, and season with salt and pepper to taste. When the roast is done, remove from oven. Let stand for 15 minutes. Just before serving, reheat the sauce if necessary. Transfer roast to a cutting board, slice evenly, and transfer to a serving platter. Serve the sauce on top of the slices or on the side. #Delish!

Caramelized Pineapple
1 large ripe pineapple
2 teaspoons butter
3 tablespoons maraschino liqueur, kirsch, or rum (optional)
3 tablespoons sugar
Squeeze lime juice (optional)

Slice skin of pineapple and remove eyes. Cut it into rounds or half-rounds about ½ inch thick. Carefully remove the core from each piece. Melt butter in a wide skillet, sprinkle some of the sugar evenly over it in a thin layer and add the pineapple. Cook over high heat until sugar has caramelized and the bottom side is richly glazed, 4 to 5 minutes. Sprinkle the tops with sugar, turn the pineapple over and cook until the second side is caramelized, another 4 to 5 minutes. Remove from pan and serve. Or add the liqueur and a squeeze lime juice, scrape the bottom, reduce until syrupy, and pour the sauce over the pineapple. #Delish!

Coconut Chicken with Pineapple Mango Salsa
¼ teaspoon salt
½ teaspoon salt
1 ¼ cups flaked coconut
1 cup chopped refrigerated mango slices (about 10 slices)
1 egg, lightly beaten
1 tablespoon lime juice
1 tablespoon vegetable oil
1/8 teaspoon cayenne pepper
14 to 16 ounces chicken breast tenderloins
2 tablespoons snipped fresh cilantro
One 8-ounce can pineapple tidbits (juice pack), drained

Preheat oven to 400 degrees. Line a large baking sheet with foil and lightly grease. Set pan aside.
In a shallow bowl, whisk together egg, oil, ¼ teaspoon salt, and cayenne pepper. Spread coconut in a second shallow bowl. Dip each piece of chicken in egg mixture, allowing excess to drop off. Coat chicken with coconut. Arrange chicken on prepared baking sheet. Bake for 10 to 12 minutes or until chicken is no longer pink. Meanwhile, make the salsa. In a medium bowl, combine pineapple, mango, cilantro, lime juice, and remaining ¼ teaspoon salt. Serve with chicken. #Delish!

Coconut Tofu with Spicy Pineapple Chutney over Rice
¼ cup plus 1 tablespoon soy sauce
½ teaspoon Chinese chili paste, or to taste
1 cup pineapple juice
1 cup unsweetened shredded coconut
1 teaspoon plain rice vinegar
15 ounces extra-firm tofu, drained
2 tablespoons canola oil
2 tablespoons mango chutney
3 tablespoons crushed canned pineapple
3 to 4 ½ cups hot cooked rice

Place the tofu on a deep-sided plate or shallow bowl. Top with a second plate and weigh down with a heavy can. Let stand for at least 15 minutes, preferably 1 hour. Drain excess water. Place tofu on cutting board and cut into 12 slices, about ½ inch thick. In a shallow casserole large enough to hold the tofu in a single layer, combine ¾ cup of the pineapple juice and ¼ cup tamari sauce. Add tofu and turn gently to coat. Let marinate 30 minutes at room temperature or cover and refrigerate 1 hour or overnight. Meanwhile, mix remaining pineapple juice and tamari with crushed pineapple, chutney, vinegar, and chili paste until completely blended. Set aside. Next, spread coconut evenly on a flat dinner plate. Coat tofu on all sides with coconut, patting it on with your fingers as necessary to make it stick. In a large skillet, heat 1 tablespoon oil over medium heat. Place half of the tofu in the skillet and cook until lightly browned, 2 to 3 minutes per side. Transfer to a covered baking dish and keep warm. Repeat with remaining tofu, browning in the remaining oil. To serve, divide rice evenly among 4 to 6 plates. Top each with a couple tofu slices. Spoon equal amounts of pineapple-chutney mixture over the tofu. Serve immediately. #Delish!

Cuban Caramel Pineapple Flan
1 cup evaporated milk
1 cup fresh pineapple chunks
1 cup pineapple juice
1 cup sugar
1 cup sweetened condensed milk
1 cup whole milk
1 teaspoon vanilla extract
3 eggs
6 egg yolks
Pinch of salt
Carefully pour hot caramel syrup into a 9-inch round glass cake pan with high sides, coating bottom and sides evenly. Set aside. Next, in a small saucepan, heat whole, evaporated, and condensed milk over low heat for 4 to 5 minutes, making sure the mixture does not start to boil. Remove from heat. Preheat oven to 325 or 350 degrees. Meanwhile, mix egg yolks and eggs with an electric mixer. Add sugar, pineapple chunks, salt, and vanilla. Then add pineapple juice. Gently mix in the milks, slowly, until thoroughly combined. Pour mixture into a blender and process at low speed to get a really smooth texture. Pour flan mixture into round caramelized and prepared pan. Set the pan into a hot-water bath. Bake in oven for 1 hour to 1 hour and 15 minutes, or until the center of the flan is firm to the touch. Remove from heat and allow to cool to room temperature Refrigerate, covered, overnight. To unmold and serve, run a sharp knife carefully around edge of the pan. Place rimmed serving plate upside down over the top of the flan, flip it over, and invert onto the serving plate. Drizzle with Cuban caramel (recipe below). Serve immediately. #Delish!

<u>Cuban Caramel:</u>
3 cups sugar
3 cups water
In a saucepan, mix sugar and water and bring to boil over medium-high heat, stirring constantly. Continue cooking and stirring until sugar has completely dissolved. Texture should be free of lumps, and thick enough to coat a wooden spoon. Cook a little longer, until syrup takes a honey color. Mixture should be between 320 and 360 degrees.

Easy Island Salsa
¼ teaspoon crushed red pepper flakes
½ cup peeled and diced jicama (¼-inch dice)
1 cup diced (¼-inch dice) fresh pineapple
1 garlic clove, minced
1 mango, peeled and cut into ¼-inch dice
1 tablespoon finely chopped cilantro
salt and freshly ground black pepper
In a small bowl, combine all ingredients and taste for seasoning. Cover and refrigerate until serving. Makes 2 cups and can be made a day in advance. #Delish!

Exotic Pineapple Beachside Martini
½ cup chopped lobster tail meat
½ cup diced red onion
1 ¼ cups finely diced mango
1 ripe tomato, diced
1 stalk lemongrass
1 tablespoon Thai fish sauce
2 ¼ cups finely diced pineapple
2 tablespoons Chile Pepper Water (recipe below)
2 tablespoons freshly squeezed lemon juice
2 tablespoons freshly squeezed lime juice
2 tablespoons freshly squeezed orange juice
2 tablespoons minced garlic
2 tablespoons olive oil
3 fresh basil leaves, julienned
3 kaffir lime leaves, julienned
3 tomatillos, husked, rinsed, and diced
Salt to taste
Cut 3 pieces from the stalk of the lemongrass, each about 1-inch long. Using flat side of a large knife or heavy skillet, flatten the pieces. Blanch the lobster meat in a saucepan of boiling salted water for 10 seconds. Remove with a wire mesh strainer and cool in an ice bath. In a bowl, combine the lemongrass, lime leaves, basil, tomato, tomatillos, pineapple, mango onion, orange juice, lemon juice, lemon juice, olive oil, Chile Pepper Water, fish sauce, garlic, blanched lobster, and salt. Marinate for 1 hour to "cook" the lobster in the fruit acids. Remove the lemongrass. To serve, divide among large martini glasses. Makes 4 servings. #Delish!

<u>For Chile Pepper Water:</u>
½ clove garlic
1 tablespoon white vinegar
1/3 cup plus 1 ¼ cups cold water
2 red Hawaiian chilies or red serrano chilies, or 1 red jalapeño, halved and seeded
2 teaspoons minced ginger
Pinch of salt
In a blender combine the 1/3 cup water, garlic, chilies, vinegar, ginger, and salt and purée until smooth. In a saucepan, bring the 1 ¼ cups of water to a boil. Add the puréed mixture and return to a boil. Remove from the heat. When cool, transfer to an airtight container. Keep refrigerated. Keeps in fridge for 1 month, and can be used as a condiment on many dishes. #Delish!

Fresh Pineapple Slaw
1 recipe pineapple vinaigrette (recipe below)
2 cups fresh pineapple, cut into ½-inch dice
2 medium carrots, peeled and shredded
2-3 teaspoons Asian sweet chili sauce (optional)
3 scallion greens, thinly sliced
4 to 5 cups thinly sliced red cabbage (about ½ head)

In a large bowl, combine cabbage, carrots, and scallions. Just before serving, generously dress the slaw with pineapple vinaigrette and stir in the diced pineapple. Drizzle Asian sweet chili sauce on top if desired. #Delish!

Granny's Pineapple Cake
¼ cup butter
½ cup brown sugar, packed firmly
1 can sliced pineapple, drained
2 packages yellow cake mix (and all needed ingredients per the package)
Maraschino cherries, drained
Line the oven with aluminum foil, shiny sides showing. Level the oven over heat and melt the butter inside. Once melted, add brown sugar, then drained pineapple slices with a cherry in the center of each slice. While butter is melting, mix the cake according to package directions. Pour the cake mix over the glaze and put lid on pan. Bake in coals for 25 minutes, until golden brown and cake tests done. Lift out of pan by edges of aluminum foil and invert onto plate. Remove foil. Serves 12. #Delish!

Grilled Pineapple and Onion Salsa
1 large red onion, cut into thick slices
1 pineapple, peeled, cored, and cut into thick rings
1 stalk lemongrass, peeled, trimmed, and minced
1 tablespoon minced fresh jalapenos or red pepper flakes
2 tablespoons chopped fresh Thai basil or mint leaves
2 tablespoons freshly squeezed lime juice
3 tablespoons olive oil
Salt and freshly ground black pepper
Heat a charcoal or gas fire grill to low heat and put the rack 4 inches from the heat source. Brush the pineapple and onion slices with the olive oil; thread them on soaked wooden skewers if they might fall through the grate. Cook, turning once or twice, until soft and slightly charred, about 8 minutes total. Remove slices, and when cool enough to handle, discard skewers and chop into bite-sized chunks, saving as much juice as possible. Place pineapple and onions in a medium bowl with chile, lemongrass, basil, and lime juice. Sprinkle with salt and pepper and stir to combine. Let sit for 5 minutes, then taste and adjust seasoning. Serve immediately or refrigerate for up to an hour. #Delish!

Happy Hummingbird Cake
¼ teaspoon ground cloves
1 ½ teaspoons vanilla
1 cup vegetable oil
1 recipe caramel butter frosting (recipe below)
1 tablespoon baking powder
1 teaspoon salt
2 cups mashed ripe bananas (about 5)
2 cups shredded, peeled raw sweet potatoes
2 cups sugar
3 cups all-purpose flour

3 eggs, lightly beaten
One 8-ounce can crushed pineapple, drained
Allow eggs to stand at room temperature for 30 minutes. Meanwhile, grease the bottoms of three 8x 1½ inch round cake pans. Line bottoms of pans with waxed paper; grease the paper. Set pans aside. Preheat oven to 350 degrees F. In large bowl, stir together flour, sugar, baking powder, salt, and cloves. Stir in egg, bananas oil, and vanilla just until combined. Fold in sweet potatoes and pineapple. Spread batter evenly in prepared pans. Bake about 30 minutes or until a toothpick inserted near the center comes out clean. Cool layers in pans on wire rack for 10 minutes. Remove layers from pans; peel off waxed paper. Cool completely on wire racks. Place one cake layer, bottom side up, on serving plate. Spread with about ½ cup of the frosting. Top with second cake layer, bottom side down. Spread with ½ cup more frosting. Top with remaining layer, bottom side up; spread top and sides of cake with remaining frosting.
For caramel butter frosting: In a large saucepan melt 1 cup butter; stir in 2 cups packed brown sugar. Bring to boiling over medium heat; stirring constantly. Cook and stir or 1 minute; remove from heat and cool for 5 minutes. Whisk in ½ cup milk until smooth. Whisk in 6 cups powdered sugar until smooth. Use immediately; frosting stiffens as it cools. #Delish!

Hawaiian Baked Beans
½ cup chopped onion
½ cup ketchup
½ cup packed brown sugar
2 tablespoons Worcestershire sauce
6 slices bacon
One 15 to 16 ounce can butter beans, rinsed and drained
One 15 to 16 ounce can kidney or pinto beans, rinsed and drained
One 15 to 16 ounce can pork and beans in tomato sauce
One 8-ounce can pineapple bits (including juice)
Preheat oven to 350 degrees. In a very large skillet cook bacon over medium heat or until crisp. Drain on paper towels, reserving 2 tablespoons drippings in skillet. Crumble bacon and set aside. Add onion to reserved drippings; cook and stir over medium heat about 4 minutes or until tender. In a 2-quart casserole combine butter beans, pork and beans on tomato sauce, kidney beans, brown sugar, can pineapple and juice, ketchup, and Worcestershire sauce. Stir in bacon and onion mixture. Bake, covered, about 35 minutes. Then remove cover and bake 10 more minutes or until bubbly around edges. #Delish!

Hawaiian Chicken Salad
¼ cup chopped macadamia nuts
¼ teaspoon salt
½ cup chopped celery (1 stalk)
½ cup chopped pineapple
½ cup thinly sliced green onions (2)
½ teaspoon finely shredded lemon peel
1 teaspoon snipped fresh basil or ¼ teaspoon dried basil, crushed
1/3 cup mayonnaise

8 ounces chopped cooked chicken or turkey (2 cups)
Bread slices or mixed salad greens (optional)

In a medium bowl combine chicken, celery, green onions, and chopped pineapple. For dressing, in a small bowl stir together mayonnaise, basil, salt, and lemon peel. Pour dressing over chicken mixture and toss gently to coat. Cover and chill for 1 to 4 hours. Before serving, add chopped macadamia nuts. Serve on bread or over salad greens. #Delish!

Hawaiian Sweet & Sour Vegetables over Rice
½ tablespoon cornstarch
½ teaspoon ground ginger
½ teaspoon salt, or to taste
1 cup fresh cubed pineapple
1 cup fresh snow peas, trimmed
1 cup sliced fresh carrots
1 cup sliced fresh green bell pepper
1 cup sliced red onion
1 cup unsweetened pineapple juice
1 tablespoon peanut oil
2 cups fresh broccoli florets
2 large cloves garlic, finely chopped
2 tablespoons plain rice vinegar
3 to 4 cups hot cooked white or brown rice
6 tablespoons light brown sugar
Freshly ground black pepper

In a small bowl, whisk together the juice, sugar, vinegar, cornstarch, and ginger until thoroughly blended. Set aside. Next, in a wok or large nonstick skillet, heat the oil over medium-high heat. Add onion, bell pepper, and garlic; cook, stirring, for 1 minute. Add the broccoli and carrots and cook, stirring, for 2 minutes. Add the snow peas and cook, stirring, 1 minute. Add the reserved liquid mixture, salt, and black pepper; bring to a brisk simmer, stirring constantly. Add the pineapple cubes and reduce the heat to medium-low. Cook, stirring, until thickened, about 3 minutes. Serve at once, over rice. #Delish!

Hibachi Pineapple Spears
2 pounds fresh pineapple, cut into thin spears
4 tablespoons brown sugar
4 tablespoons butter
Freshly ground pepper

Lay 3 to 4 spears on each of 4 pieces of foil. Top the fruit with a sprinkling of light brown sugar and a small butter dollop. Seal foil packets. Grill on both sides until the sugar melts. Open the foil and if desired, top the fruit with a little freshly ground pepper. #Delish!

High Five Freeze
¼ cup peach nectar (or juice of your choice)
½ cup crushed ice
¾ cup diced fresh pineapple (1 pineapple)
¾ cup peeled and diced mango (1 mango)
¾ cup peeled and diced papaya (1 papaya)
¾ cup peeled and diced peaches (1 peach)
¾ cup sliced banana (1 banana)
1 tablespoon honey

Place the nectar, honey, mango, papaya, banana, peach, pineapple, and ice in a blender, and mix on low speed until the mixture is blended. Continue mixing, gradually increasing the speed, until the mixture is smooth. Pour into glasses and garnish each with a pineapple spear. #Delish!

Homemade Ginger Pineapple Sherbet
½ cup pineapple juice
1 cup granulated sugar
1 tablespoon fresh lemon juice or orange juice
1 tablespoon peeled and grated fresh ginger
2 cups light cream

Mix all ingredients in a bowl. Place in a freezer until partially frozen, then mix well with a wooden spoon, or beat with a whisk. Return to the freezer until frozen. #Delish!

Island Style Couscous Salad (Vegan)
¼ chopped red onion
¼ cup golden raisins
½ cup chopped fresh cilantro
½ cup fresh lime juice
½ teaspoon ground cumin
½ teaspoon salt, plus additional to taste
1 ½ cups cubed fresh mango
1 cup cubed fresh pineapple
1 cup instant couscous, whole wheat
1 cup water
2 tablespoons canola oil
Fresh ground pepper

In a medium saucepan, bring water and salt to a boil. Stir in couscous, cover, and remove from heat. Let stand until all liquid has been absorbed, about 7 minutes. Fluff with a fork and let cool. Meanwhile, in a medium bowl, whisk together lime juice, oil, cumin, salt, and pepper. Add mango, pineapple, cilantro, onion, raisins, and toss. Add couscous and toss well to combine. Serve at room temperature. Alternatively, cover and refrigerate a minimum of 3 hours or up to 1 day and serve chilled. #Delish!

Jerk Sausage & Meatball Bites

½ cup barbecue sauce
1 teaspoon Jamaican jerk seasoning
One 16-ounce package frozen cooked meatballs
One 16-ounce package small cooked smoked sausage links
One 8-ounce can crushed pineapple, undrained

In a 4-quart slow cooker combine pineapple, barbecue sauce, and Jamaican jerk seasoning. Stir in meatballs and sausage. Cover and cook on low for 4 to 5 hours or on high for 2 to 2 ½ hours. Serve immediately. Keep warm on warm setting or low setting for up to 1 hour. Serve with toothpicks. #Delish!

Luau Salad

¼ chopped crystalized ginger
¼ cup chopped slated macadamia nuts or peanuts
½ cup shredded carrot
½ medium red onion, sliced into thin ½ rings, soaked covered in cold water for 10 minutes
½ recipe Sesame-Guava Vinaigrette
1 cup cubed fresh pineapple
1 cup egg-free fried Chow Mein noodles
1 medium mango (about 10 ounces), peeled, pitted, and cut into small chunks
1 medium red bell pepper, sliced into thin strips
1 small cucumber, thinly sliced
2 scallions, white and green parts, thinly sliced and drained
One 10-ounce bag mixed salad greens or romaine lettuce

In a large bowl, toss salad greens, mango, pineapple, ½ cup Chow Mein noodles, bell pepper, cucumber, onion, and half of the ginger until well combined. Add vinaigrette, and toss again. Divide among bowls, and garnish with carrot, scallions, nuts, and remaining ginger, and remaining Chow Mein noodles. Serve immediately. #Delish!

Ginger Sesame-Guava Vinaigrette:

¼ cup canola oil
¼ cup guava nectar
¼ cup plain rice vinegar
½ teaspoon light brown sugar, or to taste
½ teaspoon salt
1 shallot, finely chopped
1 tablespoon finely chopped fresh ginger
1 tablespoon mirin
1 tablespoon soy sauce or tamari
2 tablespoons toasted (dark) sesame oil
Freshly ground black pepper, to taste

In a small bowl, whisk together all the ingredients until thoroughly blended. Let stand at room temperature about 15 minutes to allow flavors to blend. Whisk again, and serve. #Delish!

Orange Pineapple Honey-Glazed Roast Pork

¼ cup lime juice
¼ cup pure honey
½ cup pineapple juice
¾ cup orange juice
1 canned pineapple ring
1 teaspoon ground cumin
1 teaspoon ground oregano
2 tablespoons olive oil
2 tablespoons orange zest
5 garlic cloves, peeled
One 5 to 6-pound pork shoulder, trimmed, excess fat removed

Put ¼ cup orange juice, the lime juice, and pineapple juice in a food processor. Add pineapple ring and orange zest and process a few seconds. Add another ¼ cup orange juice and the garlic cumin, oregano, and olive oil. Process to combine. Using tines of a fork, puncture pork shoulder all over so that juices penetrate. Place shoulder in a large bowl and pour fruit mixture over all. Turn shoulder several times so that juices penetrate well. Rub mixture into shoulder. Refrigerate and marinate for 1 to 2 hours, turning in marinade several times. Preheat oven to 325 degrees. Remove roast from marinade and place on rack in a roasting pan. Roast for about 1 ½ hours, or until internal thermometer reads 137 to 165 degrees. About 20 minutes before you think it will be done, blend remaining ¼ cup orange juice with honey and baste several times until a glaze appears. When done, remove from oven and cool for 20 minutes before slicing. Serve with rice and beans. #Delish!

Papaya Pineapple Strudel (Vegan)

¼ cup chopped macadamia nuts, walnuts, almonds, or pecans (optional)
¼ cup sweetened shredded coconut (optional)
½ cup pineapple preserves
1 cup chopped ripe fresh papaya (from one small papaya)
1 sheet frozen puff pastry, thawed according to package directions

Preheat oven to 375 degrees. Unfold pastry onto ungreased baking sheet. Spread evenly with preserves. Arrange half the papaya along the middle third of pastry. Sprinkle evenly with half the nuts (if using) and half the coconut (if using). Fold the third of the pastry to your left over the papaya; top pastry with remaining papaya. Sprinkle evenly with remaining nuts and coconut (if using). Fold third of the pastry to your right as far over to the other side as it will comfortably stretch, pressing the dough together where it meets to seal. Do not seal the ends. Cut about six 1-inch long slits across the top. Bake about 25 minutes, until golden. Cool on baking sheet 30 minutes. Cut into 6 slices and serve warm or at room temperature. Completely cooled strudel can be stored, covered, in refrigerator up to 1 day. For best flavor, reheat in low oven and serve slightly warm. #Delish!

Pepper-Papaya-Pineapple Chutney

1 small fresh pineapple, peeled, cored and chopped
1 medium fresh papaya, seeded, peeled and chopped
1 tablespoon peeled and minced fresh ginger
6 tablespoons granulated sugar
1 tablespoon hot Asian chili paste of choice

In a medium saucepan combine all ingredients except chili paste. Cook uncovered over medium heat for 1 hour until mixture has a syrupy consistency. Fold in the chili paste. #Delish!

Perfect Piña Colada

1 ½ ounce light rum
1 cherry
1-ounce cream of coconut
1 pineapple stick
1/3 cup cracked ice
2 ounces pineapple juice

Put rum, pineapple juice, cream of coconut, and ice into blender. Blend at high speed for 10 to 15 seconds. Pour into a tall Collins glass. Garnish with pineapple and cherry. #Delish!

Perfect Pineapple Fried Rice

¼ cup chopped cashews
¼ cup chopped fresh cilantro or basil
¼ cup raisins or currants
½ cup frozen green peas, thawed
½ cup shredded carrot
½ teaspoon mild curry powder
1 cup chopped fresh pineapple
1 fresh red or green chilies, seeded and finely chopped
2 shallots, thinly sliced
2 tablespoons peanut oil
2 tablespoons soy sauce or tamari, plus more to taste
3 cups cooked white rice, cooled
3 large cloves garlic, finely chopped
3 scallions, white and green parts, finely spiced
Salt and pepper, to taste

Mix ½ tablespoon of the oil with rice, using your fingers to separate chunks; set aside. In a large nonstick skillet or wok, heat remaining oil over medium-high heat. Add shallots, garlic, and chilies; cook, stirring constantly, until fragrant, 1 to 2 minutes. Add the peas, carrot, cashews, soy sauce, and curry powder; cook 1 minute, stirring constantly. Add the rice, pineapple, and raisins; cook, stirring constantly, until rice begins to crackle and pop, 2 to 3 minutes. Remove from the heat and toss with the scallions and cilantro, adding additional soy sauce if needed. Season with salt and pepper, and serve immediately. #Delish!

Perfectly Pineapple Vinaigrette

¼ teaspoon kosher salt
½ cup pineapple juice
1 tablespoon finely minced shallot
2 tablespoons rice vinegar
3 tablespoons canola or grapeseed oil

In a small bowl, whisk together all ingredients. Store covered in the refrigerator. #Delish!

Pickled Pineapple

½ cup granulated sugar
¾ cup cider vinegar
2 cinnamon sticks
8 whole cloves
Pinch of salt
Two (1 pound 4 ounces) cans pineapple slices with juice

Drain juice from pineapple into medium saucepan. Set pineapple slices aside. Add sugar, cinnamon, vinegar, cloves, and salt to saucepan. Bring to a full boil. Add pineapple slices and bring to a second boil. Cool. Refrigerate and serve cold or heated. Makes a great dinner side dish as well. #Delish!

Pineapple and Cantaloupe Melon Drink

½ cantaloupe melon, peeled, seeds removed, and roughly chopped
1 cup water
1 small pineapple, peeled and core removed, roughly chopped
2 tablespoons honey
4 tablespoons plain yogurt

Place pineapple and cantaloupe in a blender with yogurt, water, and honey. Blend until smooth, adding a little more water if necessary. Pour into glasses and serve. #Delish!

Pineapple and Coconut Shake

1 2/3 cups coconut milk
1 cup pineapple juice
1 cup plain yogurt
Fresh coconut as garnish (optional)
Sugar to taste

Blend coconut milk with yogurt and pineapple juice. Sweeten to taste with sugar, pour into glasses and decorate with a little fresh coconut, if desired. Serve. #Delish!

Pineapple Chess Pie
¼ cup flour
½ cup butter, softened
½ cup buttermilk
½ large extra-sweet pineapple, cleaned and sliced into 1/8" pieces, or one 20-ounce can of drained pineapple pieces
1 teaspoon vanilla
1 teaspoon vinegar
2 tablespoons dark rum
2 teaspoons lime zest
2/3 cup confectioners' sugar
3 large eggs (room temperature)

Preheat the oven to 375 degrees. In a medium bowl, whisk together the softened butter and the confectioners' sugar. Gradually whisk in the eggs one at a time. Stir in the flour, and gradually add the buttermilk, vinegar, dark rum, lime zest, and vanilla. Make sure the batter remains smooth as you incorporate the ingredients. Blind bake the pie by first placing tinfoil over the raw dough and then filling it with pie weights or beans. Bake well-rested pie shell in a 375-degree oven for 15 to 20 minutes or until it appears dry. Place the chopped pineapple in the pie shell (recipe below), and fill with the egg and buttermilk mixture. Turn the oven down to 350 degrees Fahrenheit and bake for 40 minutes or until the pie appears firm in the center. Remove from oven, cool and serve warm. #Delish!

<u>Perfect Pie Dough: (Makes 1 double crust pie)</u>
¼ shortening
¾ cup butter
1 teaspoon salt
2 ½ cups flour
3 tablespoons sugar
5-6 tablespoons ice-cold water

In a mixing bowl, combine flour, salt, and sugar. Cut butter into small cubes. Make sure to keep the butter cold. Add the butter and shortening and cut into the flour using a knife. When the flour resembles coarse sand, add the cold water. Use water sparingly, and stop adding water when the dough begins to come together. Finish bringing the dough together into a firm ball by hand, mixing as little as possible. Separate dough into two equal sized balls, and press into flat disks. Lightly flour a counter and flour the dough lightly. Roll into round disks 1/8 inch thick. Continue to flour the counter as you roll to keep from sticking. Transfer to the pie tin. Gently work dough into the bottom and sides of the pie tin. Take care not to pull the dough.

Pineapple Chili Juice
½ pineapple, peeled and halved
½ red chili, use your favorite variety
1 ½ cucumbers, halved
1 ½ oranges, peeled
Put all ingredients in the juicer, adding the chili between the pineapple and cucumbers. #Delish!

Pineapple Citrus Chutney
½ cup diced green bell pepper
½ cup diced red onion
¾ cup dark brown sugar
1 ½ cups mango chunks
1 pineapple, peeled, cut into ½ inch slices and broiled or grilled on both sides
1 tablespoon butter or margarine
1 tablespoon olive oil
1/3 cup red wine vinegar
3 garlic cloves, peeled and finely minced
3 tablespoons grated fresh ginger
Heat a medium sauté pan and add olive oil, then the butter. When sizzling, add onion, green pepper, ginger, and garlic. Cook about 2 minutes on medium-high heat. Add brown sugar and wine vinegar and bring to a boil. Cut the boiled or grilled pineapple in ½ inch pieces. Add to the mixture along with the mango chunks. Cook about 5 minutes, until flavors meld. #Delish!

Pineapple Coconut Yum Yum
<u>Bottom Crust:</u>
½ teaspoon vanilla extract
1 ½ cups all-purpose flour
1 cup macadamia nuts, chopped
2 sticks (½ pound butter), softened
2/3 cup granulated sugar
Preheat oven to 350 degrees. Cream butter and sugar until fluffy. Add vanilla, then stir in flour and macadamia nuts. Press into bottom of 13 x 9-inch pan and bake for about 10 minutes.
<u>Filling:</u>
½ cup shredded coconut
1 cup granulated sugar
1 tablespoon cornstarch
One 20-ounce can crushed pineapple with juice
Combine sugar and cornstarch in small saucepan. Add crushed pineapple with juice. Cook until thickened. Add coconut and pour over crust.
<u>Topping:</u>
½ cup granulated sugar
¼ cup all-purpose flour
8 tablespoons cold butter, cut into 8 pieces
2 cups rolled oats

Combine sugar, flour, and butter in a bowl. With a pastry cutter or 2 knives, blend mixture until the butter is the size of peas. Stir in the oatmeal. Sprinkle toping evenly over the filling. Pat down firmly. Bake at 350 degrees Fahrenheit for about 35 minutes, or until lightly browned.

Pineapple Cooler
½ teaspoon powdered sugar
1 lemon peel
1 orange spiral
2 ounces pineapple juice
2 ounces seltzer water to fill
2 ounces white wine
Put white wine, pineapple juice, powdered sugar, and 2 ounces seltzer water in tall Collins glass. Stir. Add ice cubes, fill with seltzer water, and stir again. Garnish with lemon twist and orange spiral. #Delish!

Pineapple Cucumber Mint Smoothie
1 cucumber, roughly chopped
4 ounces pineapple, peeled and roughly chopped
4 tablespoons mint leaves
Ice cubes
Using a vegetable peeler, cut thin strips of cucumber lengthways and set aside. Mix all remaining ingredients in a blender and blend until smooth. Pour into glasses and garnish with cucumber strips. #Delish!

Pineapple Key Lime Spritzers
½ cup fresh Key lime juice
½ cup superfine sugar
1 liter seltzer or sparkling water, chilled
2 cups fresh pineapple juice
Ice to serve
In half-gallon pitcher mix sugar pineapple juice, and lime juice. Refrigerate until chilled, minimum 1 hour. Just before serving, gently stir in seltzer. Serve immediately over ice. #Delish!

Pineapple Li Hing Mui
<u>Pineapple Vinaigrette:</u>
1 ½ cups diced sweet pineapple
1 ½ tablespoons balsamic vinegar
2 tablespoons olive oil
Salt to taste
<u>Balsamic Rum Syrup:</u>
¼ Cup sugar
¼ cup water
½ balsamic vinegar
1 teaspoon dark rum

8 very thin slices sweet pineapple
Li Hing Mui chutney (recipe below)
Salt and pepper to taste

To prepare vinaigrette: Combine pineapple and vinegar and purée in a blender until smooth. With machine running, slowly add olive oil until mixed. Season with salt. Refrigerate. *To prepare Rum Syrup*: In a saucepan, bring water and sugar to a boil. Boil until reduced by half. Add balsamic vinegar, return to boil, and boil until reduced by one third. Stir in rum and refrigerate until needed. Preheat oven to 200 degrees. Line baking sheet with lightly oiled parchment. Place pineapple slices on baking sheet and dry in oven for 8 hours or overnight. Serve pineapple together with Li Hing Mui Chutney. #Delish!

<u>Li Hing Mui Chutney:</u>
¼ cup balsamic vinegar
¼ cup diced macadamia nuts
¼ cup diced pineapple
¼ cup sugar
½ cup diced bananas
½ cup diced dried pitted apricots
½ cup dried diced pitted prunes
1 cinnamon stick
Juice of 1 lemon

In a saucepan, bring vinegar and sugar to a boil. Boil for 3 to 4 minutes, or until mixture thickens to syrup. Stir in the lemon juice, and cinnamon. Add prunes and apricots, and cook for 1 minute longer. When cool, stir in bananas, macadamia nuts, and pineapple.

Pineapple Marmalade

1 cup sugar
1 fresh pineapple, peeled and diced
3 cups water
Salt to taste

Leave pineapple pieces to soak in a bowl of water for about 3 hours. Drain, and discard the water. Place pineapple chunks in a large heavy saucepan with 3 cups fresh water, and boil over medium-high heat for about 25 minutes. When tender, add salt and sugar. Lower heat, and simmer for an additional 15 minutes, stirring occasionally and making sure it does not stick to the bottom of the pan. Strain mixture and transfer to a food processor. Process until very smooth. If too thick, just add water. Excellent on fresh biscuits at breakfast. #Delish!

Pineapple Mimosa

½ cup champagne or sparkling wine chilled
½ cup fresh pineapple juice
1 sugar cube
3 dashes angostura bitters
Lemon peel or mint sprig or garnish

Put sugar cube in chilled champagne glass, and saturate it with the bitters. Pour in the pineapple juice. Fill with very cold champagne, and stir gently. Garnish with lemon peel or mint sprig. #Delish!

Pineapple Mint Cooler
½ ounce white crème de menthe
1 green cocktail cherry
1 ounce lemon juice
1 pineapple stick
2 ounces gin
3 ounces pineapple juice
Iced club soda
Shake gin, crème de menthe, pineapple juice, and lemon juice well with ice. Strain into tall 14-ounce glass. Add a splash of soda and enough ice to fill glass. Stir. Garnish with pineapple stick and cherry. #Delish!

Pineapple Sherbet
¼ cup simple syrup
1 cup heavy cream
1 cup whole milk
2 cups fresh diced pineapple
2 teaspoons lemon juice
In a food processor or blender, process pineapple chunks until you have a smooth purée. In a mixing bowl, combine pineapple mixture, simple syrup, milk and cream. Add the lemon juice.
Transfer to an ice-cream maker and freeze following the manufacturer's directions. #Delish!

Pineapple Truffles
1 cup pineapple juice
1 cup toasted coconut flakes
1 egg yolk, beaten
1 tablespoon butter
1 teaspoon freshly squeezed lemon juice
2 tablespoons heavy cream
6 ounces white chocolate
In a nonreactive saucepan, bring pineapple juice to a boil. Simmer until reduced to 2 tablespoons and the concentrate has a jam-like consistency. Let cool slightly. Add butter and cream to the pan and bring to a boil Add the egg yolk and cook for 4 to 5 minutes, or until the mixture thickens. Stir in the white chocolate and lemon juice and heat, stirring, until the chocolate melts. Remove from heat, pouring the mixture into a container, and refrigerate until needed. Just before serving, place the coconut on a plate. Scoop out approximately 2 teaspoons of the chilled truffle mixture, form into a ball, and roll in the coconut. Repeat for the remaining 8 truffles. #Delish!

Pineapple Upside-Down Cake

¼ cup butter
¼ cup butter, softened
¼ teaspoon ground ginger
¼ teaspoon salt
½ cup chopped pecans, toasted
½ cup packed brown sugar
1 ½ cups all-purpose flour
1 egg
1 teaspoon vanilla
2 teaspoons baking powder
2/3 cup granulated sugar
2/3 cup milk
One 8-ounce can pineapple tidbits, drained

Preheat oven to 350 degrees. Place ¼ cup butter in a 9 x 1 ½ inch round cake pan. Place pan in oven until butter melts. Stir in brown sugar. Arrange pineapple and pecans in pan; set aside. In a medium mixing bowl stir together flour, granulated sugar, baking powder, salt, and ginger. Add milk, ¼ cup softened butter, egg, and vanilla. Beat with mixer on low until combined. Beat on medium for 1 minute. (Batter might still be lumpy). Spread batter in prepared pan. Bake for 30 to 35 minutes or until a toothpick inserted near center comes out clean. Cool in pan on wire rack for 5 minutes. Loosen sides of cake; invert onto plate. Cool for 30 minutes; serve warm. #Delish!

Pineapple-Brown Sugar Glazed Chicken Breasts

½ cup unbleached all-purpose flour
1 ½ cups plus 2 tablespoons pineapple juice
1 medium shallot, minced
1 tablespoon Dijon mustard
1 tablespoon distilled white vinegar
1 tablespoon vegetable oil
1/3 cup light corn syrup
1/8 teaspoon red pepper flakes
2 tablespoons brown sugar
4 (10 to 12 ounce) bone in, skin-on split chicken breasts, trimmed
Salt and pepper to taste

Preheat oven to 375 degrees. Whisk 1 ½ cups pineapple juice, corn syrup, brown sugar, mustard, vinegar red pepper flakes, 1/8 teaspoon salt and 1/8 teaspoon pepper together in medium bowl. Set aside. Place flour in a shallow dish. Pat chicken dry and season with salt and pepper. Working with one chicken breast at a time, coat the chicken with flour, shaking off excess. Heat oil in a 12-inch oven-safe skillet over medium-high heat until just smoking. Brown chicken on both sides, 5 to 8 minutes per side. Transfer chicken to a plate. Pour off all but 1 teaspoon of fat from the pan. Return pan to medium heat, add the shallot, and cook until softened, about 2 minutes. Increase heat to high and add pineapple juice mixture. Simmer until syrupy and reduced to about 1 cup, 6 to 10 minutes. Remove skillet from heat and tilt to one side. Using tongs, roll each chicken breast in pooled glaze to coat evenly and place, skin-side down, in the skillet. Next, transfer skillet to the oven and bake until thickest part of the chicken registers 160 degrees Fahrenheit, about 25 to 30 minutes, turning chicken skin-side up half-way through cooking. Transfer chicken to platter and let rest for 5 minutes. Meanwhile, return skilled to high eat, and cook glaze stirring constantly, until thick, about 1 minute. Remove pan from heat and whisk in remaining 2 tablespoons pineapple juice. Spoon glaze over each breast and serve. #Delish!

Pineapple-Coconut Milk Drink
1 banana
1 teaspoon orange flower water
2 cups chopped fresh pineapple
One 15-ounce can unsweetened coconut milk
Splash rum (optional)
Blend all ingredients plus ½ cup water together and pour over ice. #Delish!

Polynesian Paralysis
¼ cup guava juice
¼ cup passion fruit juice
¼ cup unsweetened pineapple juice
1 ½ tablespoons Bacardi light rum
1 ½ tablespoons Captain Morgan's spiced rum
1 ½ tablespoons Malibu coconut-flavored rum
1 ½ tablespoons Myer's dark rum
1 maraschino cherry
1 mint sprig
1 pineapple wedge, for garnish
Ice

This drink is meant to be layered, and drunk with a straw from the bottom of the glass without stirring or mixing the layers. Place the ice in a large hurricane glass. Pour in the coconut-flavored rum and pineapple juice. Carefully and slowly pour in the spiced rum and passion fruit juice to create a second layer. Pour in the light rum and guava juice for a third layer. Finally, float the dark rum on top. Add cherry and mint sprig. Garnish the glass with the pineapple wedge. Serve with a straw. #Delish!

Pressed Cuban Ham and Pineapple Sandwiches
½ cup (4 ounces) cream cheese, softened
12 slices cooked ham (baked, sweet, or honey)
2 teaspoons butter
8 slices whole wheat, cinnamon or pumpernickel
One 8-ounce can pineapple rings, drained or 4 large slices of fresh pineapple
Spread cream cheese on flour slices of bread. Layer each with a pineapple ring, and pile high with thinly sliced ham. Top with remaining bread slice. Heat butter in large skillet over medium heat until it bubbles slightly. Place sandwiches in skillet, and press each with a clean heavy smaller skillet, spatula, or plate. Turn over to brown the other side, and continue to cook for about 4 minutes. Remove from skillet with spatula, and serve immediately. #Delish!

Rosy Fruit Cocktail
1 pound dark sweet cherries
1 pound seedless green grapes
3 pounds peaches
3 pounds pears
5 ¼ cup Light Syrup (recipe below)
One 2-pound pineapple

For light syrup: In large saucepan cook and stir 1 ¼ cups sugar, 5 cups water, and if desired on 3-inch cinnamon stick over medium heat until sugar dissolves. Remove and discard cinnamon. Keep syrup hot, but not boiling. While simmering, wash fruit. Slice the bottom stem and the green top off the pineapple. Stand pineapple on cut end and slice off skin in wide strips. Discard skin. To remove eyes cut diagonally around fruit, following pattern of the eyes making narrow wedge-shape grooves. Cut away as little of the meat as possible. Cut pineapple in half lengthwise; place pieces cut sides down and cut lengthwise again. Cut off and discard center core from each quarter. Finely chop pineapple. Measure 3 cups. Peel, pit, and cut peaches into cubes. Measure 8 ½ cups peaches. Peel, core and cut pears into cubes. Measure 6 ½ cups pears. Halve and pit cherries. Measure 2 ½ cups cherries. Remove stems from grapes. Measure 3 cups grapes. Next, in a 6-quart pot combine pineapple, peaches, pears, cherries, and grapes. Add hot syrup; heat to boiling. Pack hot fruit and syrup into hot, sterilized jars, leaving ½ inch headspace. Wipe jar rims; adjust lids. Process filled jars in a boiling water canner for 20 minutes. Remove jars from canner; cool on wire racks. #Delish!

Rum, Mango, and Pineapple Relish
¼ cup finely diced scallions
¼ cup golden rum
½ cup finely chopped yellow onion
1 cup peeled and chopped mango
1 red bell pepper, seeded and finely diced
1 ripe pineapple, peeled and cut into small pieces
1 tablespoon granulated sugar
2 tablespoons sherry vinegar

Heat sugar and vinegar in a medium saucepan over low heat. Add pineapple, mango, onion, and pepper and allow to simmer for about 3 minutes. Add the scallions and rum; combine well. Cook for another 3 to 4 minutes. Serve warm or cold. #Delish!

Slow-Cooker Sweet and Sour Sticky Ribs
¼ cup dark brown sugar
¼ teaspoon red pepper flakes
1 medium onion chopped
1 red bell pepper, stemmed, seeded, and chopped
2 tablespoons minced fresh cilantro leaves
2 tablespoons tomato paste
2 tablespoons vegetable oil
5 tablespoons rice vinegar
6 medium garlic cloves, peeled and crushed

6 pounds baby back ribs or St. Louis-style spareribs
6 tablespoons soy sauce
One 12-ounce jar apricot jam
One 6-inch piece fresh ginger, peeled and sliced into ¼ inch rounds
One 6-ounce can frozen pineapple juice concentrate
Salt and pepper

Pulse onion, bell pepper, garlic, and ginger together in food processor until finely chopped, about 8 pulses. Heat oil in a nonstick skillet over medium-high heat until shimmering. Add vegetables and tomato paste and cook, stirring often, until vegetables are softened and lightly browned, 8 to 10 minutes. Stir in the apricot jam, pineapple juice concentrate, soy sauce, brown sugar, ¼ cup vinegar, and red pepper flakes; bring to a simmer, and cook until slightly thickened, about 5 minutes. Pat ribs dry with paper towels and season with salt and pepper. Transfer to slow cooker and arrange standing upright with meaty side against interior wall. Pour sauce over ribs, cover, and cook on low until meat is tender, 4 to 5 hours. Transfer ribs to carving board, tent with foil and let rest for 20 minutes. Let cooking liquid settle for 5 minutes, then gently tilt slow cooker and remove as much fat as possible using large spoon. Strain sauce through fine mesh strainer into medium saucepan. Bring sauce to a simmer and cook until measures 2 cups, about 15 to 20 minutes. Next, stir remaining tablespoon vinegar into sauce and season with salt and pepper. Slice ribs and toss with sauce and cilantro. Transfer to warm platter and serve. #Delish!

Spiced Pork Tenderloin with Pineapple Salsa
¼ Teaspoon cayenne pepper
½ teaspoon grated lime zest plus 2 tablespoons juice
1 jalapeño chile, stemmed, seeded, and minced
1 teaspoon ground allspice
2 cups pineapple, cut into ½ inch pieces
2 tablespoons chopped fresh cilantro
2 teaspoons ground coriander
2 teaspoons ground cumin
Salt and pepper
Two 12-ounce pork tenderloins, trimmed

Preheat oven to 475 degrees. Set wire rack inside rimmed baking sheet and place on oven rack. Combine coriander, cumin, allspice, ½ teaspoon salt, ¼ teaspoon pepper, and cayenne in bowl. Pat pork dry with paper towels and coat evenly with spice mixture. Transfer pork to preheated wire rack and roast until meat registers 145 degrees Fahrenheit, about 20 minutes, flipping halfway through cooking. Transfer to carving board, tent loosely with aluminum foil, and let rest for 5 minutes. Meanwhile, combine pineapple, cilantro, jalapeño, and lime zest and juice in bowl. Season with salt and pepper to taste. Slice pork into ¼ inch thick slices and serve with salsa. #Delish!

Taiwan-Style Vegetable Wraps with Spicy Pineapple Sauce

¼ cup chopped peanuts
1 cup bean sprouts
1 cup shredded carrots
1 cup snow peas
12 (8-inch) round rice papers
2 scallions, white and green parts, thinly sliced
Pineapple Five-Spice Dipping Sauce (recipe below)
Salt and freshly ground black pepper, to taste

Bring a medium stockpot filled with salted water to a boil over high heat. Add snow peas and blanch until barely softened, 30 seconds. Drain and rinse under cold-running water until cooled. Drain well. Next, in medium bowl, toss together snow peas, sprouts, carrots, scallions, peanuts, 2 tablespoons of the dipping sauce, salt, and pepper until thoroughly combined. Let stand about 10 minutes and toss again. Prepare bowl of warm water large enough in which to dip the rice papers. Working with one at a time, dip the rice paper in the warm water 8 to 10 seconds, or until it begins to soften. Transfer to a flat work surface. Working quickly, put about ¼ cup vegetable filling on a wrapper. Fold the bottom of the wrapper up over the filling, and then fold each side toward the center. Roll from the bottom to the top of each roll, as tightly as you can without ripping the wrapper. Wrap in plastic wrap to keep from drying out. Repeat with remaining papers and filling. Serve at room temperature, with the remaining dipping sauce. Alternatively, refrigerate a minimum of 2 hours, or overnight, and serve chilled or return to room temperature. #Delish!

<u>Pineapple Five-Spice Dipping Sauce:</u>
¼ cup plain rice vinegar
¼ cup soy sauce or tamari
½ cup pineapple preserves, at room temperature
½ teaspoon toasted (dark)sesame oil
2 teaspoons Chinese five-spice powder
Fresh ground black pepper

In small bowl, whisk together all ingredients until well combined. Serve at room temperature. Sauce can be stored, covered, in refrigerator up to one week. Return to room temperature before serving.

Tropical Spice Pork Tacos

¼ Teaspoon ground black pepper
¼ teaspoon ground cumin
1 ½ teaspoons salt
1/8 teaspoon ground cloves
2 dried chipotle chilies, brushed clean
2 slices fresh pineapple
2 tablespoons white vinegar
3 ancho chilies, brushed clean
4 medium garlic cloves, peeled
One 3-pound boneless pork butt
One 6-ounce can pineapple juice
<u>Tacos:</u>

Fresh cilantro sprigs
Lime wedges
Minced white or red onion
Sour cream
Twelve (6-inch) soft corn tortillas, warmed

For the Pork: Adjust an oven rack to the middle position and heat the oven to 350 degrees F. Place ancho and chipotle chilies on a baking sheet and toast in oven until fragrant and puffed, about 6 minutes. Remove chilies from the oven and cool. When cool enough to handle, seed and stem chilies, then transfer to a medium bowl. Cover with hot tap water and soak, stirring occasionally, until soft but not mushy, about 20 minutes. Drain chilies and transfer to a blender discarding water. Add pineapple juice, garlic, salt, cumin, pepper, and cloves, and puree until smooth, 30 to 60 seconds. Lay pineapple slices in bottom of an 8-inch square baking dish. Place pork roast on top of pineapple and coat with ½ cup of pureed chile mixture. Cover tightly with foil and roast until pork is tender and falls apart when prodded with a fork, about 2 ½ hours. Remove pork from oven, loosen foil and let rest 15 minutes. Using two forks, shred pork and pineapple in dish discarding large pieces of fat. Stir vinegar into remaining ½ cup pureed chile mixture, then stir into shredded pork to taste. Assemble tacos by spooning a small amount of shredded pork into center of each warm tortilla and serve with remaining chile mixture, cilantro, onion, sour cream, and lime wedges. #Delish!

White Crème Pineapple Rum

1-ounce white crème de menthe
2 cups cracked ice
2 cups fresh pineapple chunks
2 fresh mint sprigs (for garnish)
2 tablespoons chopped fresh mint leaves
3 ounces simple syrup
5 ounces dark rum

Add ice, pineapple, rum, simple syrup, mint leaves, and crème de menthe to a blender. Blend well. Pour into 2 good-sized glasses, and garnish with a mint sprig. #Delish!

**Thank you for your purchase!
May you enjoy and be well!**

ABOUT THE AUTHOR

I am a Tennessee native and a connoisseur of great tastes. My culinary delights are inspired by my Southern roots.

I am from cornbread and cabbage, fried chicken and Kool-Aid soaked lemon slices.

I am from hen houses, persimmon trees and juicy, red tomatoes on the vine.

I am from sunflowers growing wild in summer and homemade ice cream in the winter.

I am from family reunions, blue collar men, happy housewives, and Sunday dinners.

I am from spiritual folks who didn't always get it right, but believed in the power of prayer – and taught it to their kids.

I am from the hottest of hot summers and kids running barefoot and free through thirsty Tennessee grass.

I am from a grandmother who sang gospel that was magic…song drenched air would tumble from her lungs, leap into your spirit and make you feel fantastic things.

I am from hard, heartfelt lessons about living and kitchens full of the perfume of love.

♥♥♥ This book is from my heart to yours. ♥♥♥

Find more cookbooks online at http://www.tinyurl.com/sodelishdish.
For freebies & new book announcements, follow @SoDelishDish on social media!

Scan with your smartphone!

Printed in Great Britain
by Amazon